Little RIDDLERS

Surrey Voices

Edited By Kelly Scannell

First published in Great Britain in 2018 by:

YoungWriters

Young Writers
Remus House
Coltsfoot Drive
Peterborough
PE2 9BF
Telephone: 01733 890066
Website: www.youngwriters.co.uk

All Rights Reserved
Book Design by Ashley Janson
© Copyright Contributors 2018
SB ISBN 978-1-78896-787-7
Printed and bound in the UK by BookPrintingUK
Website: www.bookprintinguk.com
YB0372L

FOREWORD

Dear Reader,

Are you ready to get your thinking caps on to puzzle your way through this wonderful collection?

Young Writers' Little Riddlers competition set out to encourage young writers to create their own riddles. Their answers could be whatever or whoever their imaginations desired; from people to places, animals to objects, food to seasons. Riddles are a great way to further the children's use of poetic expression, including onomatopoeia and similes, as well as encourage them to 'think outside the box' by providing clues without giving the answer away immediately.

All of us here at Young Writers believe in the importance of inspiring young children to produce creative writing, including poetry, and we feel that seeing their own riddles in print will keep that creative spirit burning brightly and proudly.

We hope you enjoy riddling your way through this book as much as we enjoyed reading all the entries.

CONTENTS

Independent Entries

Kyrese (6)	1

Culvers House Primary School, Mitcham

Angel Ponan (7) & Zhirara	2
Jeshaun Myles-Robert Vanriel (7)	3
Vishakan Prathap (7)	4
Lexi-Mai Bulmer (7)	5
Lenny Macquire (5)	6
Samuel Rider (7)	7
Myles McLean (7)	8
Ceana Gabrielle Nacino (7)	9
Divine Teixeira (6)	10
Marcus Iyekekpolor (6)	11
Srinesh Mohanram Naidu (6)	12
Fred Olarotimi Bright (7)	13
Kizzi Bailey (6)	14
Ewomazino Amaria Obata (6)	15
Abdul Jallali (6)	16
Faith Owolabi (6)	17
Ethan Amoamah Plange (6)	18
Jaeda Ramgeet (6)	19
Kristin Enachi (5)	20
Ava Botting (6)	21
Alexis Musiyiwa (6)	22
Rafif Mahdi (6)	23
Lorenzo Belbin-Chappenden (6)	24
Nadia Zoya Khan (6)	25
Sashwina Suthakaran (6)	26
Alex Young (6)	27
Patsy Meechan (6)	28
Ismat Owoseni (6)	29
George Banerji (6)	30
Alexander Dighton (5)	31
Joy Ugobere (6)	32
Aiden Blake (6)	33
Eliana Stott (6)	34
Jack Hawkins (6)	35
Freya Dighton (5)	36
Maham Khalid (6)	37
Casey James Harvey-Raggett (5)	38
Freddie Boylan (6)	39
Si'an Campbell (5)	40
Aarush Variya (5)	41
Reuben Browne (5)	42
Liam Dale (5)	43
Joao Antonio Ramalho Martins (6)	44
Madison Muir (6)	45
David Martins Costa (6)	46
Luca Benjafield (6)	47

Harris Primary Academy Haling Park, Croydon

Alec Bound (7)	48
Chad Latagan (7)	49
Enzo Garcia (6)	50
Hadiyah Allybuccus (7)	51
Casey McMurrough (7)	52

Homefield Preparatory School, Sutton

Prayaan Sharma (7)	53

Meath Green Infant School, Horley

Amara Isabella Okeke (6)	54
Isabelle Violet Card (7)	55
Emily Gibbins (7)	56
Max Lewis (6)	57
Bluebelle Rose Towse (7)	58
Caitlin Sarah-Louise Brennan (6)	59
Charlie Colwill (7)	60
Lucie Rodd (7)	61
Lily Gould (7)	62
Evie Higton (7)	63
Timothy Shew (7)	64
Oscar Steven Denyer (7)	65
Ella Chiedza Mlambo (7)	66
Brandon Sam Arndt Lewis (7)	67
Robyn Woolston (7)	68
Frankie Holt (7)	69
Kaitlin Eddens (7)	70
Sophie Bonnar (7)	71
Maisie Anne Brown (6)	72
Nathaniel Chadwick (7)	73
Joseph Denton (6)	74

Milford School, Milford

Fife Angas (6)	75
Ben Bolton	76
Frederic Everett Hardy (6)	77
Cooper Linden (5)	78
Fletcher Holden (6)	79
Ella Welton (6)	80
Juliet Meneely (5)	81
George Moore	82
Archie Millard (6)	83
Harry Dodd (6)	84
Summer	85
Robin Pinnells (5)	86
Harry John Moir (6)	87
Sebastian Bernard Norman (5)	88
Chloe Stanton (6)	89
Seb Radwanski	90
Harlow Blu-Deborah Cork (6)	91

Lucy Davidson	92
Sebastian Bonard (6)	93
Bethany Gibbons (6)	94
Joel Kenny Bullock (5)	95
Amy Mason (6)	96
Dexter Jordan (6)	97
Dylan Sheikh-Thompkins (6)	98
Daisy Martin (6)	99
Olivia Loveland (5)	100
Matilda Adrienne Isa Slaughter (6)	101
Mia Smith (5)	102
Max Neale (6)	103
Isla Neesham (5)	104
Ethan Carter	105
Reuben Jean Hardy (6)	106

New Monument Primary Academy, Maybury

Lily Mahoney (7)	107
Ifra Khadijah Nazir (7)	108
Michael Hendry (7)	109
Maryam Rahmani (6)	110
Zain Rasul (7)	111
Amina Nazir (6)	112
Ahmad Ali Zafar (6)	113
Musa Hussain (7)	114

South Farnham Infant School, Lower Bourne

Sophia Jasmine Guwy (7)	115
Fleur Hadden (7)	116
Sasha Schrader (7)	117
Freddie Batchelor (6)	118
Clara Anthony (7)	119
Jamie Neatherway (6)	120
Sakura Fukushima-Choularton (7)	121
Cillian Michael Lee (7)	122
Lily Isabel Trossell (7)	123
Eliza Keightley (7)	124
Maisie Beames (6)	125

Surbiton High Boys' Preparatory School, Surbiton

Henry James Edward Sage (7)	126
Will RG Kemmish (7)	127
Xander Stewart (7)	128
Harry Alford (8)	129
Toby Batchelor (5)	130
Kailan Yathaven (7)	131
Gabriel Welsh (7)	132
Arjan Aggarwal (6)	133
Harry Grosvenor (6)	134
Fraser Black (5)	135
Freddie Slade (7)	136
Neal Hemnani (6)	137
Archie Burnett (6)	138
Konrad Granberg (7)	139
Dimitri Ciais (7)	140
Faaris Nasir (7)	141
Jack Houlahan (6)	142
William Britton (7)	143
Rohan Gidoomal (7)	144
Nicholas Shahverdian (5)	145
Aarav Shetty (6)	146
Thomas So (7)	147
Marcus Pandilharatna (7)	148
Raj Hundal (7)	149
Oliver Hill (5)	150
Eyad Hammad (7)	151
Zihao Xu (7)	152
Raphie Nicholas Dawe Benning-Prince (7)	153
Jason Wang (7)	154
Yusuf Rangwala (6)	155
Teddy Williams (6)	156
Henry Frederick Brian Whiting (7)	157
Theo T (7)	158
Aidan Pearson (7)	159

THE POEMS

Dangerous Animals

I'm as scary as a tiger.
I have a long tongue.
Did you know that I can swallow a woman in one gulp?
Did you know that I eat mice?
Did you know that I hide in the trees to look for my prey?
Can you believe that I sleep in the day time?
What am I?

Answer: A snake.

Kyrese (6)

The Fluffy One

I have a bushy, adorable tail,
I am a cutie pie.
I live in a sunny field
Where people can feed me.
I have whiskers, legs, a mouth and a head.
I am not a cat, but I am like a kitten.
I am a herbivore.
I eat lots of leaves and plants,
I also eat vegetables.
I am as fluffy as a puppy.
What do you like about me?
What a mysterious animal I am!
What am I?

Answer: A bunny.

Angel Ponan (7) & Zhirara
Culvers House Primary School, Mitcham

The Dangerous Creature

I have a furry mane around my neck.
I run as fast as a panther.
I live in the dark, scary jungle.
I hide in bushes and behind trees to hunt my prey.
I live with my pride in stony places.
Did you know my roar is as loud as a speaker?
I eat juicy meat.
I am as strong as a whale.
What am I?

Answer: A lion.

Jeshaun Myles-Robert Vanriel (7)
Culvers House Primary School, Mitcham

God's Snake Or What?

I'm a long, slithery snake.
My habitat is India with its large homes and bumpy roads.
My long head points upwards.
I eat every animal and humans and my other prey.
My movement is called slithering.
You can sometimes visit me in the zoo.
I have lots of space in my tummy.
What am I?

Answer: An anaconda.

Vishakan Prathap (7)
Culvers House Primary School, Mitcham

Cute Animals

I sometimes live at Pets at Home
And sometimes in a cage.
I can be small, medium or large.
My baby can be as furry as a pillow or as sleek as silk.
I am good at looking after my big, beautiful house.
I have to be walked daily.
I love to eat meat.
I am happy every day.
What am I?

Answer: A puppy.

Lexi-Mai Bulmer (7)
Culvers House Primary School, Mitcham

What Am I?

I have four legs.
I have grey skin.
I eat plants because I am a herbivore.
I am a mammal.
I live in a jungle or the zoo.
I make a weird sound.
I am covered in grey.
I slip in mud.
When I slip in mud, I turn brown.
I have a trunk.
I am big.
What am I?

Answer: An elephant.

Lenny Macquire (5)
Culvers House Primary School, Mitcham

A Cute Animal

I have a long tongue, but I'm not a lizard.
I am really warm and have lots of fur.
You might find me in the really green park.
I am as cute as a rabbit.
My tail wags all the time when I'm in the park.
I eat meat.
When I'm born, I have no fur.
What am I?

Answer: A dog.

Samuel Rider (7)
Culvers House Primary School, Mitcham

Scary Or Not?

I am brown.
I am slimy and scary.
I have an extremely long tongue, but I'm not a frog.
What do you think?
Sometimes, I have beautiful patterns on my back, but I'm not a lizard.
I can eat a whole bone in one gulp.
I am as long as a building.
What am I?

Answer: A snake.

Myles McLean (7)
Culvers House Primary School, Mitcham

Hopping Animal

I am as round as a cute, little animal.
I don't eat meat, I eat vegetables.
I come at Easter and hop around.
If you can tell who I am, you'll find my name down below.
People love me because I am the cutest animal in the world.
What am I?

Answer: A bunny.

Ceana Gabrielle Nacino (7)
Culvers House Primary School, Mitcham

Sharp Feline

I am furry.
I have sharp claws and pointy nails.
I hear well.
I roar like a lion.
I drink milk.
I can move super fast.
I can roar really loud.
I jump but I am not a jumpy rabbit.
Did you know I live in a warm home?
What am I?

Answer: A cat.

Divine Teixeira (6)
Culvers House Primary School, Mitcham

What Am I?

I have four legs.
I am an omnivore, I eat meat and plants.
I am covered in black fur.
I mostly fight animals.
I am strong.
I live in the zoo.
I am a mammal.
I am from a movie.
I fight a lot of my enemies.
What am I?

Answer: A panther.

Marcus Iyekekpolor (6)
Culvers House Primary School, Mitcham

Are You Cheeky?

I take hats from people.
I can swing tree to tree.
Sometimes, snakes come to eat me.
I live in trees.
You can find me in the jungle.
Elephants are my friends.
I like to eat bananas.
What am I?

Answer: A monkey.

Srinesh Mohanram Naidu (6)
Culvers House Primary School, Mitcham

What Am I?

I have sharp teeth.
I am as fierce as a lion, but I am not a tiger.
Do you know that I can swallow someone with one gulp?
I eat seals and fish.
I live in the wavy ocean.
What am I?

Answer: A shark.

Fred Olarotimi Bright (7)
Culvers House Primary School, Mitcham

What Am I?

I am pink and brown.
I eat fish underwater.
I have pink all over me.
I am a carnivore and I only eat meat.
I have four legs.
I open my mouth very wide.
What am I?

Answer: A hippo.

Kizzi Bailey (6)
Culvers House Primary School, Mitcham

What Am I?

I can fly really high.
Sometimes, I like to eat apples.
I have soft hair.
My skin is white.
I have a horn on my forehead.
I have a crown on my head.
What am I?

Answer: A unicorn.

Ewomazino Amaria Obata (6)
Culvers House Primary School, Mitcham

What Am I?

I have four legs.
I am black and orange, but the bottom of my tail is white.
I am a carnivore and I eat meat.
I am a mammal.
I live in the garden.
What am I?

Answer: A fox.

Abdul Jallali (6)
Culvers House Primary School, Mitcham

What Am I?

I have legs.
I am a herbivore.
I am a mammal.
I hang on trees.
I am black and white.
I eat plants and leaves.
I eat bamboo leaves.
What am I?

Answer: A panda.

Faith Owolabi (6)
Culvers House Primary School, Mitcham

What Am I?

I am a herbivore.
I eat grass.
I have four legs.
I have sharp horns.
I am grey and brown.
I am a mammal.
I can jump high.
What am I?

Answer: I am a gazelle.

Ethan Amoamah Plange (6)
Culvers House Primary School, Mitcham

What Am I?

I have four legs.
I have soft fur.
I have pointy ears.
I eat meat that means I am a carnivore.
I bark when the yellow doorbell rings.
What am I?

Answer: A dog.

Jaeda Ramgeet (6)
Culvers House Primary School, Mitcham

What Am I?

I have four legs.
I am a mammal.
I am pink and grey.
I am small and cute.
I roll over in the mud.
I eat grass and meat.
What am I?

Answer: I am a pig.

Kristin Enachi (5)
Culvers House Primary School, Mitcham

What Am I?

I am magical.
I can fly.
I am beautiful.
I love hay.
I drink cold water.
I move quickly.
I have shiny teeth.
What am I?

Answer: I am a unicorn.

Ava Botting (6)
Culvers House Primary School, Mitcham

What Am I?

I have four legs and I jump.
I am cute and have long ears.
I eat yummy carrots.
I live on a lovely farm.
I am a soft mammal.
What am I?

Answer: A rabbit.

Alexis Musiyiwa (6)
Culvers House Primary School, Mitcham

What Am I?

I have four legs to jump.
I eat carrots.
I have long ears.
I am brown.
I am small.
I am an herbivore.
I am furry.
What am I?

Answer: A rabbit.

Rafif Mahdi (6)
Culvers House Primary School, Mitcham

What Am I?

I have soft fur.
I have four legs.
I am spotty and yellow.
I eat red meat.
I am a mammal.
I live in the green jungle.
What am I?

Answer: A cub.

Lorenzo Belbin-Chappenden (6)
Culvers House Primary School, Mitcham

What Am I?

I have soft and cuddly fur.
I am a baby.
I have four legs.
I have pointy ears.
I live in a house.
I drink milk.
What am I?

Answer: A kitten.

Nadia Zoya Khan (6)
Culvers House Primary School, Mitcham

What Am I?

I have four legs.
I am covered in soft fur.
I am a carnivore because I only eat meat.
I am a mammal.
I purr loudly.
What am I?

Answer: A cat.

Sashwina Suthakaran (6)
Culvers House Primary School, Mitcham

What Am I?

I have a beak.
I have feathers.
I have wings.
I can fly.
I am black and red.
I like to peck wood.
What am I?

Answer: A woodpecker.

Alex Young (6)
Culvers House Primary School, Mitcham

What Am I?

I have one colossal horn.
I am beautiful.
I am magical.
I am sparkly white.
I have four red legs.
What am I?

Answer: I am a unicorn.

Patsy Meechan (6)
Culvers House Primary School, Mitcham

What Am I?

I have four legs.
I eat lettuce.
I am a mammal.
I live in the river.
I have soft fur.
I am brown.
What am I?

Answer: A beaver.

Ismat Owoseni (6)
Culvers House Primary School, Mitcham

What Am I?

I growl and bark when somebody is coming.
I have black and yellow fur.
I am a carnivore.
I like walks.
What am I?

Answer: A puppy.

George Banerji (6)
Culvers House Primary School, Mitcham

What Am I?

I have two legs.
I have defeated a Pikachu.
I have two other forms.
I am the form after a Pikachu.
What am I?

Answer: A Raichu.

Alexander Dighton (5)
Culvers House Primary School, Mitcham

What Am I?

I have four legs.
I am big and grey.
I am an herbivore because I eat fruit.
I live in the zoo.
What am I?

Answer: An elephant.

Joy Ugobere (6)
Culvers House Primary School, Mitcham

What Am I?

I have four legs.
I am black and white.
I eat bamboo.
I am a mammal.
I live in the jungle.
What am I?

Answer: A panda.

Aiden Blake (6)
Culvers House Primary School, Mitcham

What Am I?

I have four legs.
I am a herbivore.
I eat leaves.
I'm grey.
I have a trunk.
What am I?

Answer: An elephant.

Eliana Stott (6)
Culvers House Primary School, Mitcham

What Am I?

I am an herbivore.
I live in Africa in the jungle.
I have four legs.
I eat leaves.
What am I?

Answer: An elephant.

Jack Hawkins (6)
Culvers House Primary School, Mitcham

What Am I?

I have two legs.
I am black.
I eat insects.
I am a mammal.
I live in dark caves.
What am I?

Answer: A bat.

Freya Dighton (5)
Culvers House Primary School, Mitcham

What Am I?

I have four legs.
I am black.
I eat plants.
I am a mammal.
I live underground.
What am I?

Answer: A mole.

Maham Khalid (6)
Culvers House Primary School, Mitcham

What Am I?

I have four legs.
I have a long neck.
I have little horns.
I have a head.
What am I?

Answer: A giraffe.

Casey James Harvey-Raggett (5)
Culvers House Primary School, Mitcham

A Hard Shell

I have a hard shell.
I have a soft body.
My shell is scaly.
I eat plants.
What am I?

Answer: A turtle.

Freddie Boylan (6)
Culvers House Primary School, Mitcham

What Am I?

I eat meat.
I live in the jungle.
I have no legs.
I slither on the ground.
What am I?

Answer: A snake.

Si'an Campbell (5)
Culvers House Primary School, Mitcham

What Am I?

I have very sharp teeth.
I am a carnivore.
I eat meat.
I am very fierce.
What am I?

Answer: A lion.

Aarush Variya (5)
Culvers House Primary School, Mitcham

What Am I?

I have two legs.
I am an animal.
I am brown.
I swing in the trees.
What am I?

Answer: A monkey.

Reuben Browne (5)
Culvers House Primary School, Mitcham

What Am I?

I have zero legs.
I am a carnivore.
I live in the sea.
What am I?

Answer: A killer whale.

Liam Dale (5)
Culvers House Primary School, Mitcham

What Am I?

I have four legs.
I am covered in fur.
I like to purr.
What am I?

Answer: A cat.

Joao Antonio Ramalho Martins (6)
Culvers House Primary School, Mitcham

What Am I?

I have four legs.
I can't fly.
I like to purr.
What am I?

Answer: A cat.

Madison Muir (6)
Culvers House Primary School, Mitcham

What Am I?

I have two legs.
I have wings.
I eat insects.
What am I?

Answer: A bat.

David Martins Costa (6)
Culvers House Primary School, Mitcham

What Am I?

I have two legs.
I am black.
I can fly.
What am I?

Answer: A bird.

Luca Benjafield (6)
Culvers House Primary School, Mitcham

Smoke Billower

I blow out smoke.
I have tall, big and strong wheels.
I have a driver and lots of passengers.
I have five chairs in a row for you to sit.
I go stormingly, quickly, very fast.
It's a challenge to drive me.
You have to make me go to my highest top speed before I stop!
What am I?

Answer: A steam train.

Alec Bound (7)
Harris Primary Academy Haling Park, Croydon

Wordy!

I can either have loads of things in me or not.
There are loads of different styles of me.
I can be funny or not.
Maybe I can be pretty or handsome or I can be very ugly.
You can also make me at home or school.
They always use me in school.
What am I?

Answer: A book.

Chad Latagan (7)
Harris Primary Academy Haling Park, Croydon

The Mystery

I spray paint my teacher's rear end!
I jump on people's heads if they're sunbathing.
My friend made Captain Underpants.
We went back in time!
I have a best friend.
Who am I?

Answer: Harold Hutchins.

Enzo Garcia (6)
Harris Primary Academy Haling Park, Croydon

Fly High

I'm something that can fly high.
I fly above the sky.
I have two wings and sharp edges on my wings.
I can fly all around the world.
What am I?

Answer: A plane.

Hadiyah Allybuccus (7)
Harris Primary Academy Haling Park, Croydon

Cute Hoppers

I am cute and fluffy.
I hop so high.
I eat vegetables.
I roam in the field.
I can be your pet.
What am I?

Answer: A rabbit.

Casey McMurrough (7)
Harris Primary Academy Haling Park, Croydon

Arctic Flippers

I can live on water and I can live on land.
I have tusks like an elephant and whiskers like a cat.
I can be a cow, bull or calf.
I can clap but I don't have hands.
I'm afraid of orcas and polar bears.
Who am I?

Answer: A walrus.

Prayaan Sharma (7)
Homefield Preparatory School, Sutton

Terrific Girl

She is very funny.
Her heart is full of honey.
She is so sweet, she can never be beat.
Why is she so funny you ask, because she always makes me laugh.
She is like a real friend.
I hope this riddle will never end.
She is like the stars in the sky, you ask me just why?
She is terrific like the stars, no one knows if we're on Mars.
If it is a sunny day, she'll be the path to our way.
Who is she?

Answer: Thea.

Amara Isabella Okeke (6)
Meath Green Infant School, Horley

The Fast Hopper

I'm a fast hopper, but a slow stopper.
I have a baby in my pouch and when she falls, she says, "Ouch!"
I jump really high up in the sky.
I live in Australia where it's nice and hot.
I don't have stripes, but do I have dots?
I have a big, long tail so my balance doesn't fail.
What am I?

Answer: A kangaroo.

Isabelle Violet Card (7)
Meath Green Infant School, Horley

Flying High

I am an insect.
There are between 15,000 and 20,000 species of me.
I can fly.
I like flowers.
I eat nectar from flowers.
I attach my eggs to leaves.
I have four wings.
My wings are brightly coloured.
The pattern on my wings is unique.
I emerge from a chrysalis.
What am I?

Answer: A butterfly.

Emily Gibbins (7)
Meath Green Infant School, Horley

Happy

I am the time of year when people visit the pier.
Build sandcastles in the sun and have lots of fun.
Eat ice cream in the park, the dogs like to bark.
Barbecues outside, long, sunny bike rides.
Shades are on, flip flops too.
This time of year there's lots to do.
What am I?

Answer: Summer.

Max Lewis (6)
Meath Green Infant School, Horley

The Magical Legend

My silvery wings help me take flight.
My four-legged body is snow white.
Rainbow is the colour of my beautiful hair!
I'm the magical relative of the horse (or mare).
I have a sparkly, golden, spiral horn
And I like to chew the grass from the lawn.
What am I?

Answer: A unicorn.

Bluebelle Rose Towse (7)
Meath Green Infant School, Horley

Sweet Dreams

I have four legs, but I cannot walk.
I have a head, but I cannot think.
I have springs, but you should not jump on me.
I work while you rest.
I have monsters under me and angels over me.
You are happy to see me at the end of the day.
What am I?

Answer: A bed.

Caitlin Sarah-Louise Brennan (6)
Meath Green Infant School, Horley

Eating Machine

I come from China.
I have fluffy, black and white fur.
I have black patches surrounding my eyes.
I'm like a cuddly teddy bear.
My favourite food is bamboo.
I love spending my day eating lots and sitting.
What am I?

Answer: A panda.

Charlie Colwill (7)
Meath Green Infant School, Horley

The Animal Question!

I am quite small.
Lots of us can have something different.
I have a curved back.
I have eight legs.
I don't like water, but sometimes I get wet.
I am all over the world.
I make cobwebs.
What am I?

Answer: A spider.

Lucie Rodd (7)
Meath Green Infant School, Horley

Drip, Drip, Drop

I fall down quickly from the high, dark sky.
My sound is drip, drop, drip, drop.
I look like little drops of water.
I make continuous ripples in ponds.
I make muddy puddles bigger.
I am wet.
What am I?

Answer: Rain

Lily Gould (7)
Meath Green Infant School, Horley

Best Friends

I have a pointed horn.
I'm indescribable.
Some people think I don't exist.
My name is Princess Celestia in My Little Pony.
Some people love me!
I'm kind of like a rainbow.
What am I?

Answer: A unicorn.

Evie Higton (7)
Meath Green Infant School, Horley

Peck, Peck, Peck

I like to peck seeds and grubs.
I don't usually fly, but I can.
I make a lot of noise.
I have an enormous tail.
I have lots of eyes.
I am usually colourful, often green and blue.
What am I?

Answer: A peacock.

Timothy Shew (7)
Meath Green Infant School, Horley

Fossilised Creatures

I have sharp teeth.
I have a long tail.
I have strong, scaly skin.
I have small arms.
I am a carnivore.
I am so, so scary.
I lay eggs.
People have found fossils of me.
What am I?

Answer: A T-rex.

Oscar Steven Denyer (7)
Meath Green Infant School, Horley

Skippy's Jumping Power

I live in Australia.
I like to jump around.
I have a furry pocket.
I can stand on two legs.
Some call me Roo.
My ears are larger than rabbit ears.
I balance on my tail.
What am I?

Answer: A kangaroo.

Ella Chiedza Mlambo (7)
Meath Green Infant School, Horley

Tree Climber

I have pointed teeth.
I have sharp claws.
I can climb trees.
I have deadly eyes.
I creep through the jungle.
I'm a part of the cat family.
What am I?

Answer: A black panther.

Brandon Sam Arndt Lewis (7)
Meath Green Infant School, Horley

My Fluttery Friend!

I am small.
I have wings.
I fly gracefully through the sky.
My wings are see-through.
I am cute.
I have a body.
I can speak.
I am magical.
What am I?

Answer: A fairy.

Robyn Woolston (7)
Meath Green Infant School, Horley

Nature

I am big and small
And all different sizes and colours.
Squirrels jump on me.
I live indoors and outdoors.
Birds nest in me.
There are loads of me
What am I?

Answer: A tree.

Frankie Holt (7)
Meath Green Infant School, Horley

Cold Fun!

I am cold.
You can make me.
I can disappear.
You can only play with me in the winter.
I do not like the sunshine.
You can dress me up.
What am I?

Answer: A snowman.

Kaitlin Eddens (7)
Meath Green Infant School, Horley

High Tide

It's cold and warm.
Oil can be found below.
Moves in and out.
Can be rough.
Separates some countries.
People relax next to it.
What is it?

Answer: The sea.

Sophie Bonnar (7)
Meath Green Infant School, Horley

Soft And Fluffy

I live in a hole underground.
I eat lots of carrots.
I have two big, floppy ears.
I have very soft, fluffy fur.
I hop a lot.
What am I?

Answer: A bunny rabbit.

Maisie Anne Brown (6)
Meath Green Infant School, Horley

The Fierce Roar

I have four legs.
I hunt for my prey.
I have two eyes.
I have black stripes.
I have sharp claws.
I have a fierce roar.
What am I?

Answer: A tiger.

Nathaniel Chadwick (7)
Meath Green Infant School, Horley

What Am I?

I am very hot.
You won't like me.
You would not like to touch me.
I shoot out of something.
What am I?

Answer: Lava.

Joseph Denton (6)
Meath Green Infant School, Horley

The Blazing Sun

I can see some beautiful flowers.
Butterflies are gliding in the air.
Sausages are popping on the barbecue.
You can have ice cream.
Lovely bees are flying around.
The blazing sun shines on you.
What season is it?

Answer: Summer.

Fife Angas (6)
Milford School, Milford

Joyful

It is windy.
You need to build scarecrows.
Conkers on the floor.
Cutting golden corn.
Acorns falling off trees.
You find bugs crawling on the ground.
Leaves falling too.
What season is it?

Answer: Autumn.

Ben Bolton
Milford School, Milford

What Am I?

It can be rainy or sunny.
You can see gold baby chicks in the sun.
You can go in a paddling pool.
You can have ice cream.
You can smell flowers.
You can go places.
What season is it?

Answer: Spring.

Frederic Everett Hardy (6)
Milford School, Milford

Family Time

Children are going to the beach
To play and swim in the sea.
People sunbathing when it is hot.
Families go camping to have a barbecue.
Everyone goes on holiday.
What season is it?

Answer: Summer.

Cooper Linden (5)
Milford School, Milford

Fun Times

It is hot.
Make new friends.
Blossom falling from the trees.
Some plants grow.
Hold chicks.
Frogspawn in the water.
Buds growing with water and sun.
What season is it?

Answer: Spring.

Fletcher Holden (6)
Milford School, Milford

Snowy December

Throwing balls of soft cold ice.
Making funny snowmen.
Drinking brown, bubbly hot chocolate.
Having fun with my friends.
Waiting for Santa to visit.
What season is it?

Answer: Winter.

Ella Welton (6)
Milford School, Milford

The Walk

I had chocolate ice cream on the beach.
I went on holiday to Dubai.
I could see the sun shining in the sky.
I went for a walk when the sun was shining.
What season was it?

Answer: Summer.

Juliet Meneely (5)
Milford School, Milford

Freezing Cold

It is good for the polar bears.
You wear warm clothes.
You can throw snow.
Mostly you stay in.
Sit and you get very cold.
It sometimes rains.
What season is it?

Answer: Winter.

George Moore
Milford School, Milford

Leaves

The scarecrow is scaring the birds.
The leaves are falling from the trees.
Red, yellow and orange colours everywhere.
Warm toffee apples sticky to eat.
What season is it?

Answer: Autumn.

Archie Millard (6)
Milford School, Milford

The Smooth Nut

I can hear crunching leaves.
Scarecrows are scaring crows.
Smooth acorns and rough bark on trees.
I can smell the corn.
I can jump on leaves.
What season is it?

Answer: Autumn.

Harry Dodd (6)
Milford School, Milford

Fun Times With Your Family

Fluffy, yellow chicks are born.
It rains sometimes.
Sometimes, it is warm.
There is pink blossom on the trees.
Tadpoles are swimming around.
What season is it?

Answer: Spring.

Summer
Milford School, Milford

Eggs Are Hatching

The chicken eggs are hatching.
The rain is pouring down.
The plants are growing.
I can hear birds singing.
I can feel wool on sheep.
What season is it?

Answer: Spring.

Robin Pinnells (5)
Milford School, Milford

The Sunny Day

There are children playing on the beach,
Building sandcastles.
It is sunny.
I can feel the sun on my cheeks.
I can taste ice cream.
What season is it?

Answer: Summer.

Harry John Moir (6)
Milford School, Milford

Freezing

You have snowball fights.
You wear woolly jumpers.
You make snowmen.
You don't see bees and wasps.
You wear woolly hats.
What season is it?

Answer: Winter.

Sebastian Bernard Norman (5)
Milford School, Milford

The Colourful Butterflies

I can hear fluttering wings.
It feels a bit hot.
I can smell sweet flowers.
I can see daffodils.
Baby lambs are being born.
What season is it?

Answer: Spring.

Chloe Stanton (6)
Milford School, Milford

Fun Heat

You can go to the green hills.
Go camping.
There are noisy thunderstorms.
You can go to the beach.
You can go on holiday.
What season is it?

Answer: Summer.

Seb Radwanski
Milford School, Milford

People Making Snowmen

I can see children wearing warm clothes like woolly hats and jumpers.
It is very cold, so we have to wear gloves.
We build snowmen.
What season is it?

Answer: Winter.

Harlow Blu-Deborah Cork (6)
Milford School, Milford

Cold Days

Animals are hatching from their really good, cosy, warm eggs.
Flowers are growing really high.
It is raining really, really badly.
What season is it?

Answer: Spring.

Lucy Davidson
Milford School, Milford

Flowers

I can see beautiful flowers.
This is when flowers grow.
I can hear little chicks hatch.
There are tadpoles and frog spawn.
What season is it?

Answer: Spring.

Sebastian Bonard (6)
Milford School, Milford

Hot And Cold

The sun is hot.
Butterflies come out.
Flowers start to grow.
Sunbathing and swimming.
It's when animals wake up.
What season is it?

Answer: Spring.

Bethany Gibbons (6)
Milford School, Milford

The Bubblegum Ice Cream

It is hot and sunny.
The sun is shining.
The bubblegum ice cream is melting.
The tent is up.
We are going camping.
What season is it?

Answer: Summer.

Joel Kenny Bullock (5)
Milford School, Milford

What Am I?

You go somewhere.
Relaxing time.
Floppy, flowery hats.
Ice cream melting.
People sweating.
Boiling hot sun.
What season is it?

Answer: Summer.

Amy Mason (6)
Milford School, Milford

Windy Season

The conkers fall down.
It is windy.
You build a scarecrow.
The leaves fall down.
They make a crunchy floor.
What season is it?

Answer: Autumn.

Dexter Jordan (6)
Milford School, Milford

Digging

Digging in the deep, soft sand.
Having noisy barbecues.
Licking cold ice cream.
Going in the cool paddling pool.
What season is it?

Answer: Summer.

Dylan Sheikh-Thompkins (6)
Milford School, Milford

The Hot Weather

On the beach, people are hot.
Mums put sun cream on their children.
Ice creams are melting.
Sunglasses are on!
What season is it?

Answer: Summer.

Daisy Martin (6)
Milford School, Milford

Leaves

I can see the acorns falling from the trees.
Red, yellow and orange leaves on the ground.
Crunchy leaves.
What season is it?

Answer: Autumn.

Olivia Loveland (5)
Milford School, Milford

Ice Lollies

The sun is as bright as a light.
It is hot.
The trees are green.
Children play and eat ice lollies.
What season is it?

Answer: Summer.

Matilda Adrienne Isa Slaughter (6)
Milford School, Milford

The Hot Burning Thing

It's as hot as lava.
Don't look straight at it.
Butterflies come out.
People sunbathe.
What season is it?

Answer: Summer.

Mia Smith (5)
Milford School, Milford

The Sound Of The Season

I can see the red lights on the Christmas tree.
I can hear Jingle Bells.
I can smell Christmas pudding.
What season is it?

Answer: Winter.

Max Neale (6)
Milford School, Milford

Guess Me!

I can hear the lambs bleating.
I can see eggs hatching.
The flowers are growing.
What season is it?

Answer: Spring.

Isla Neesham (5)
Milford School, Milford

What Am I?

Family days out.
Walks along the river.
Sizzling sausages and family going out.
What season is it?

Answer: Summer.

Ethan Carter
Milford School, Milford

King Of The Cold

I am cold.
I make you cold.
Snow may fall.
What season is it?

Answer: Winter.

Reuben Jean Hardy (6)
Milford School, Milford

The Fly Eater

I have eight legs.
I make a trap that you can't see.
I could be in your house.
I'm a skinny bug.
I'm dark black however you're not.
Also, I eat delicious flies.
What am I?

Answer: A spider.

Lily Mahoney (7)
New Monument Primary Academy, Maybury

The Animal That Flies

I have beautiful wings.
I have two wings.
I am very colourful.
I'm not a bird.
I come from a caterpillar
And I turn into something else.
What am I?

Answer: A butterfly.

Ifra Khadijah Nazir (7)
New Monument Primary Academy, Maybury

Asia Riddle

I am very small, but I am not Singapore.
My population is 358,098.
I am a country is Asia.
My ratio is 1:2.
My flag was adopted in 1959.
What country am I?

Answer: Brunei.

Michael Hendry (7)
New Monument Primary Academy, Maybury

The Grower

I look very pretty.
I am all pretty colours.
I live in any country.
I need sun.
Bees get food from me.
I need water to survive.
What am I?

Answer: A flower.

Maryam Rahmani (6)
New Monument Primary Academy, Maybury

Apple Eater

I have a queen.
My nest is underground.
I am little but I am strong.
I have a colony.
I collect food from people's houses.
What am I?

Answer: An ant.

Zain Rasul (7)
New Monument Primary Academy, Maybury

The Fluffy Thing

I have four legs.
I live on a farm.
I am soft a wool.
I eat grass but I am not a cow.
I am fluffy as a cloud.
What am I?

Answer: A sheep.

Amina Nazir (6)
New Monument Primary Academy, Maybury

The Dangerous Animal

Green is my colour
And my teeth are sharp.
I eat fish.
Also, I've got a tail.
I'm not a fish.
What am I?

Answer: A crocodile.

Ahmad Ali Zafar (6)
New Monument Primary Academy, Maybury

The Small Creature

I fly and have babies.
I am black and yellow.
I collect things from flowers.
Plus, I die easily.
What am I?

Answer: A bee.

Musa Hussain (7)
New Monument Primary Academy, Maybury

Nessst

I am a carnivore and I eat once every two weeks.
I can grow up to eight feet long.
I have patterned skin and a triangular-shaped head.
When I am a baby, I can't rattle.
I am venomous and can be aggressive, but don't mean to hurt you.
I regulate my own temperature and hibernate in winter.
What am I?

Answer: A rattlesnake.

Sophia Jasmine Guwy (7)
South Farnham Infant School, Lower Bourne

What Am I?

I'm slippery and steep.
You need to climb a ladder to get to the top of me.
I'm lots of fun.
You would find me at a playground or in a garden
Or even at a water park.
Children use me on beautiful days for adventure.
I come in many different sizes,
Sometimes small and sometimes tall.
What am I?

Answer: A slide.

Fleur Hadden (7)
South Farnham Infant School, Lower Bourne

Feathery Friends

We always fly around in the sky
To Africa or Spain.
At least, we met an aeroplane!
We hatch from an egg.
Luckily, we have a cosy nest to sleep in.
We wait until our mother comes with a juicy worm.
We have two legs, but no hands.
We can still wave.
What are we?

Answer: Sparrows.

Sasha Schrader (7)
South Farnham Infant School, Lower Bourne

High In The Sky

Where can I be found?
I'm found on the ground.
When hit, I fly high,
Way up in the sky.
I am used to play a sport
Not on a tennis court.
I'm black and white.
Am I a kite?
I land in a goal
That's attached to a pole.
What am I?

Answer: A football.

Freddie Batchelor (6)
South Farnham Infant School, Lower Bourne

Tea, Table Or Dessert

You scoop me up and stuff me in
For cereals, mousse and ice cream too.
My favourite friends are Knife and Fork.
We all lie around with our pal, Plate.
I come in lots of different sizes.
You can even hang me from your nose.
What am I?

Answer: A spoon.

Clara Anthony (7)
South Farnham Infant School, Lower Bourne

Sleep Deep

My face is like a triangle.
But my base is like a rectangle.
I am very easy to break apart.
I am hard to put up at the start.
You sleep in me,
But you need a torch to see,
Especially if you need a wee!
What am I?

Answer: A tent.

Jamie Neatherway (6)
South Farnham Infant School, Lower Bourne

Magical Night

I run really fast.
Only a few people will see me.
I have a sparkling tail.
I disappear in the sky after I run.
I come out at night.
I am as bright as a moon.
Whoever sees me makes a wish.
What am I?

Answer: A shooting star.

Sakura Fukushima-Choularton (7)
South Farnham Infant School, Lower Bourne

Ding Dong Time

I have a face, but no eyes.
I have two hands, but cannot touch.
I tick and I tock.
I have numbers, but they aren't big.
I come in different shapes and sizes.
I tell things, but do not talk.
What am I?

Answer: A clock.

Cillian Michael Lee (7)
South Farnham Infant School, Lower Bourne

Stripy Magic!

High in the sky, you can see me.
I don't come out that often,
But I sparkle when I do.
Some say I am magic
And some wish upon me too.
Some just like my colours like red, green and blue.
What am I?

Answer: A rainbow.

Lily Isabel Trossell (7)
South Farnham Infant School, Lower Bourne

March Madness

I have long, pointy ears.
I have powerful hind legs.
I run 45mph.
I live above ground.
I will be found in the countryside.
I am known for my boxing.
What am I?

Answer: A hare.

Eliza Keightley (7)
South Farnham Infant School, Lower Bourne

Magical Powers

I am magical.
I make wishes come true.
I can fly.
I have a mane.
I have white fur.
I have one horn.
What am I?

Answer: A unicorn.

Maisie Beames (6)
South Farnham Infant School, Lower Bourne

Soaring In The Sky!

I have wings, but they are not feathery.
I have wheels, but I am not a trolley.
I have windows, but I am not a house.
I need fuel, but I am not a car.
I have a nose, but I cannot smell.
I have an aisle, but I am not a theatre.
I have lots of tables, but I am not a cafe.
I have a captain, but I am not a boat.
What am I?

Answer: An aeroplane.

Henry James Edward Sage (7)
Surbiton High Boys' Preparatory School, Surbiton

Riddle

I am not a dinosaur, but many think I am.
I had huge teeth.
I appeared after the famous Jurassic era.
I was mighty and strong.
I was sixty feet long.
I died in the last ice age because my food was all gone.
I was once king of the seas,
But now my bones rest in the hot Sahara.
What am I?

Answer: A megalodon shark.

Will RG Kemmish (7)
Surbiton High Boys' Preparatory School, Surbiton

Munch Bunch

I'm yellow, curved and great.
I'm usually bought with three or four mates.
My insides are white
And you can eat me bite by bite.
For breakfast, lunch or dinner,
Nothing keeps you thinner
In a cake, on a tree,
Monkeys like to eat me.
What am I?

Answer: A banana.

Xander Stewart (7)
Surbiton High Boys' Preparatory School, Surbiton

Take A Seat!

I have legs, but I can't run!
I have a back, but I can't bend.
I'll support you, but I won't cheer you on.
When you read, I'll hold you.
When you are tired, I will be with you.
I come in many shapes and sizes.
What am I?

Answer: A chair.

Harry Alford (8)
Surbiton High Boys' Preparatory School, Surbiton

Night Sky

I am yellow.
I am bright.
You can see me in the sky at night.
I am high up in the sky.
Sometimes, I fly by.
I am boiling hot
And I am really far away.
I am big, but I look small.
There are millions of us all.
What am I?

Answer: A star.

Toby Batchelor (5)
Surbiton High Boys' Preparatory School, Surbiton

Nature

I am from the East.
I was taught by a man whose name rhymes with who.
I am green in colour, but I can be gold.
I fight for good with the help of my friends.
With me, there are six.
I am a combination of nature strengths.
Who am I?

Answer: Lloyd.

Kailan Yathaven (7)
Surbiton High Boys' Preparatory School, Surbiton

Hidden Danger

I once would have dazzled you, but now you can't see me.
I'm very heavy, but surprisingly small.
Don't come too close or you'll get sucked in!
You'll find me in a place that reminds you of chocolate.
What am I?

Answer: A black hole.

Gabriel Welsh (7)
Surbiton High Boys' Preparatory School, Surbiton

Sport

I am played every four years.
Thirty-two countries compete to win me,
But only one team can hold me.
I have been living in Germany.
This year, I will be played in Russia.
The whole world unites to watch me.
What am I?

Answer: *The World Cup.*

Arjan Aggarwal (6)
Surbiton High Boys' Preparatory School, Surbiton

Tommy Kay

I am red, but not hot.
I am smooth, but sharp.
I am tomatoey, but not round.
I am squeezy, but not huggable.
I am yummy for the young, but not for old people.
I go well with chips, but not with salad.
What am I?

Answer: *Tomato ketchup.*

Harry Grosvenor (6)
Surbiton High Boys' Preparatory School, Surbiton

Engine Power

I have one level or two.
Ring my bell and I will stop for you.
I am big and red and strong.
I carry lots of people all day long.
I drive on a road, but I am not a car.
I take people to places near and far.
What am I?

Answer: A bus.

Fraser Black (5)
Surbiton High Boys' Preparatory School, Surbiton

What Am I?

You mix me before I'm made.
I could be a mask in a parade.
I am sticky and wet.
I am quite fragile when dry.
You can paint me lots of colours
And make different shapes and sizes.
What am I?

Answer: Papier-mâché.

Freddie Slade (7)
Surbiton High Boys' Preparatory School, Surbiton

Carrot Crazy

I am fluffy.
I am white.
I have long ears
And I live up to four years.
I eat carrots.
I live in burrows
And in homes.
I am fast,
Even though I came last against the tortoise.
What am I?

Answer: A hare.

Neal Hemnani (6)
Surbiton High Boys' Preparatory School, Surbiton

The Pass

I play a sport.
I sneak past defenders so I don't get caught.
I wear a kit.
I have to be fit.
I kick a ball and try not to fall.
My team has to win or else we end up in the bin.
What am I?

Answer: A footballer.

Archie Burnett (6)
Surbiton High Boys' Preparatory School, Surbiton

What Am I?

I have a handle, but cannot turn.
I am hot, but do not burn.
I can pour, but not run.
You can put a drink in me.
I come in different colours and sizes.
I am a pot with a letter.
What am I?

Answer: A teapot.

Konrad Granberg (7)
Surbiton High Boys' Preparatory School, Surbiton

Bouncy Ball

I have fluffy legs.
I have a soft, cuddly tail.
I like to chase the ball.
I have a sparkling collar.
I look like a big teddy bear.
I like to bark.
What am I?

Answer: Dimitri's dog, Bonzai.

Dimitri Ciais (7)
Surbiton High Boys' Preparatory School, Surbiton

Water City

I am a city in Italy.
I have lots of water.
There are no cars here.
People travel on boats.
I have many bridges.
I have special boats called gondolas.
Which city am I?

Answer: Venice.

Faaris Nasir (7)
Surbiton High Boys' Preparatory School, Surbiton

Noinim

We have a very big family with thousands of brothers.
We're all a bit crazy.
Our favourite food is yellow in colour, as are we.
We love to serve our evil boss.
What are we?

Answer: Minions.

Jack Houlahan (6)
Surbiton High Boys' Preparatory School, Surbiton

Meat-Eater

Meat-eater.
It has sharp teeth.
It can swim and walk.
It lives in hot countries.
It likes salty water.
It is ugly.
It eats people.
What is it?

Answer: A saltwater crocodile.

William Britton (7)
Surbiton High Boys' Preparatory School, Surbiton

The Golden Boot!

I'm named after a prophet.
I'm very expensive.
I'm number 11.
They call me The Pharaoh.
I'm good on grass
And extremely fast.
Who am I?

Answer: Mohamed Salah.

Rohan Gidoomal (7)
Surbiton High Boys' Preparatory School, Surbiton

What My Mummy Calls Me!

I am good at climbing.
I love bananas.
I live in the jungle.
I have a very long tail.
I am brown and furry.
There are lots of species of me.
What am I?

Answer: A monkey.

Nicholas Shahverdian (5)
Surbiton High Boys' Preparatory School, Surbiton

Bagheera

I look like a cat.
That is black.
That is furry.
That lives in the jungle.
That has a snake-like tail.
That has four bear-like paws.
What am I?

Answer: A black panther.

Aarav Shetty (6)
Surbiton High Boys' Preparatory School, Surbiton

Double Vision

I may be hot.
I may be cold.
I may be bought.
I may be sold.
I may be flat.
I may be curvy.
I may be clear.
I may be blurry.
What am I?

Answer: A television.

Thomas So (7)
Surbiton High Boys' Preparatory School, Surbiton

My Riddle

I squirm and squiggle.
I wriggle and jiggle.
When you pull me, I squeal.
I'm warm with mud.
I have a stalk.
I'm in Harry Potter.
What am I?

Answer: A mandrake.

Marcus Pandilharatna (7)
Surbiton High Boys' Preparatory School, Surbiton

The Flying Thing

I can float.
I'm not a boat.
Sometimes I'm white.
Sometimes I'm bright.
You can try to touch,
But you can't smell me much.
What am I?

Answer: A cloud.

Raj Hundal (7)
Surbiton High Boys' Preparatory School, Surbiton

Friends And Families

I come in styles.
I have a window.
I have a number on me.
I have a door.
I am big or small.
I have a roof.
I might have a chimney.
What am I?

Answer: A house.

Oliver Hill (5)
Surbiton High Boys' Preparatory School, Surbiton

Yummy, Yellow, Fruity

I am a fruit.
My colour is yellow.
I can be green too.
You need to peel me to eat me.
You can mix me to drink me.
My skin is slippery.
What am I?

Answer: A banana.

Eyad Hammad (7)
Surbiton High Boys' Preparatory School, Surbiton

Zihao's Riddle

I have a bushy tail.
I have a person on my back.
I eat a lot of grass.
I have long, brown hair.
I live on a farm.
I am a mammal.
What am I?

Answer: A horse.

Zihao Xu (7)
Surbiton High Boys' Preparatory School, Surbiton

Little Nipper

I live in the sea.
I have sharp teeth.
I am small.
I hunt in shoals with my family.
I can eat big fish,
But I am not a shark.
What am I?

Answer: A piranha.

Raphie Nicholas Dawe Benning-Prince (7)
Surbiton High Boys' Preparatory School, Surbiton

The Greatest Magician

I can be small.
I can be big.
I can be beautiful or like a pig.
I am cold.
I love the cold.
Hot magic helps me disappear.
What am I?

Answer: A snowman.

Jason Wang (7)
Surbiton High Boys' Preparatory School, Surbiton

Cheesy Treat

I am round or square.
I'm covered with cheese.
I can be plain or not plain.
I can be thin or thick.
I am popular and yummy.
What am I?

Answer: A pizza.

Yusuf Rangwala (6)
Surbiton High Boys' Preparatory School, Surbiton

Roarrrrr!

I kill to eat.
I am a predator.
I have a long mane.
My babies are called cubs.
I have big feet.
I live in the zoo.
What am I?

Answer: A lion.

Teddy Williams (6)
Surbiton High Boys' Preparatory School, Surbiton

What Am I?

I am small and fluffy.
I am incredibly cute.
I am nocturnal.
My teeth never stop growing
So I am always gnawing.
What am I?

Answer: A hamster.

Henry Frederick Brian Whiting (7)
Surbiton High Boys' Preparatory School, Surbiton

Fun Food

I come from Italy.
I am round.
I can be hot or cold.
I can be thick or thin.
I can be vegetarian or a meat feast.
What am I?

Answer: A pizza.

Theo T (7)
Surbiton High Boys' Preparatory School, Surbiton

What Am I?

I'm very soft, but quite big.
I am black and white.
I'm a type of bear.
I am an animal in a movie.
What am I?

Answer: A panda.

Aidan Pearson (7)
Surbiton High Boys' Preparatory School, Surbiton

YoungWriters
Est.1991

YOUNG WRITERS INFORMATION

We hope you have enjoyed reading this book – and that you will continue to in the coming years.

If you're a young writer who enjoys reading and creative writing, or the parent of an enthusiastic poet or story writer, do visit our website **www.youngwriters.co.uk**. Here you will find free competitions, workshops and games, as well as recommended reads, a poetry glossary and our blog.

If you would like to order further copies of this book, or any of our other titles, then please give us a call or visit **www.youngwriters.co.uk**.

Young Writers
Remus House
Coltsfoot Drive
Peterborough
PE2 9BF
(01733) 890066
info@youngwriters.co.uk